Ships
at Sea

Geoff Thompson

Contents

Ships

There are many kinds of ships.

ocean liner

cargo ship

aircraft carrier

Ships can carry very big loads across the sea.

Ships are much bigger
than boats.
The first ships and boats
were made of wood.
Some of them had sails.

Now ships are made of steel.
They have engines
that help them move through the water.

Ships and boats long ago...

Early Egyptian boats

These boats had one big sail
and were used to sail
to nearby countries.

Viking longboats

Longboats
were made of wood.
They were very strong
in heavy seas.

Sailing ships

These ships had many sails
and could go a long way
across the ocean.

Ships today...

Ocean liners are much faster
than sailing ships.
They use engines.

Ocean liners

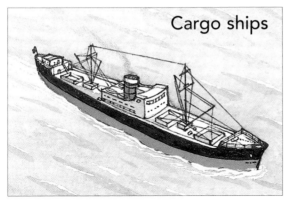
Cargo ships

These ships take huge loads
from one place to another.

Submarines are ships
that can go under the sea.

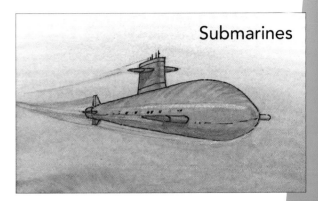
Submarines

Sailing the Seas

Long ago, sailing ships
were the only way to cross the sea.

Painting of an old sailing ship

These ships had sails to catch the wind.
The wind blew into the sails.
This pushed the ship forward.

Sailing ships could not move
if there was no wind.

Ocean Liners

Today, ocean liners carry lots of people across the sea.

People go on vacations at sea on ocean liners.

Ocean liners
have many cabins.
Cabins are small rooms
where people sleep.

Ocean liners have swimming pools and stores.
Some have playrooms for children, too.

Submarines

A submarine is a ship
that can go deep down under the sea.

Submarines can float on top of the water, too.

Submarines can move quickly
through the water
because they are long and thin
and have round ends.

DID YOU KNOW?

Some submarines
can stay under the water
for up to 60 days.

Cargo Ships

Cargo ships take big loads
from one place to another.

This cargo ship is a container ship.
Containers are loaded onto the ship.
They are full of all kinds of cargo.

This cargo ship
is an oil tanker.
Oil tankers
are very long.
Inside,
they have big tanks
filled with oil.

DID YOU KNOW?

Some oil tankers are so long
that sailors have to ride a bike
to get from one end
to another.

Hovercraft

A hovercraft is a special kind of ship.
It can go over water and up onto land.

A hovercraft sits on a huge air cushion.

Propellers on top of the hovercraft
help to push it forward.

Big hovercraft take people
on short, fast trips across the sea.

Ferries

Ferries take people on trips
across rivers and lakes.
Sometimes they go across the sea
from one island to another.

Some big ferries carry cars and trucks.
The cars and trucks
get into the ferry through big doors
at one end of the ferry.
They are parked in a special place
called a hold.

Aircraft Carriers

Aircraft carriers are very big ships.
Planes can take off and land
from the runways on aircraft carriers.

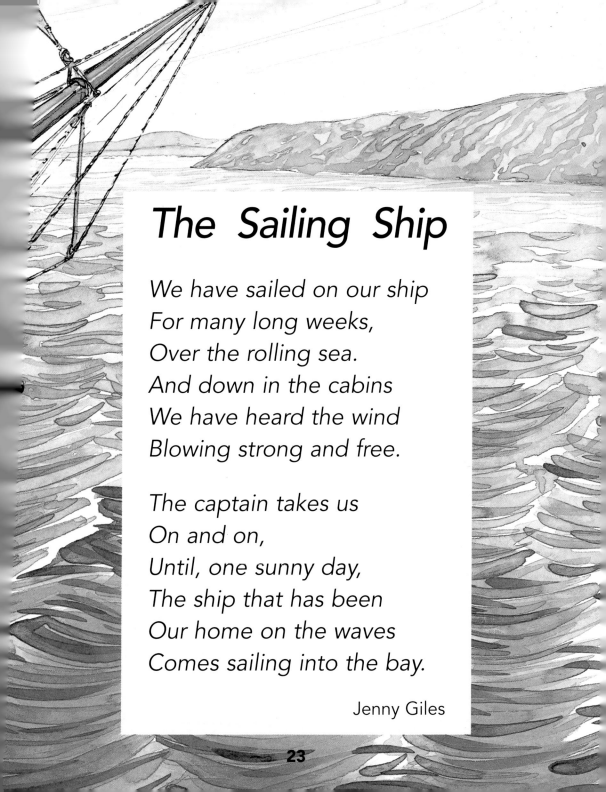

The Sailing Ship

We have sailed on our ship
For many long weeks,
Over the rolling sea.
And down in the cabins
We have heard the wind
Blowing strong and free.

The captain takes us
On and on,
Until, one sunny day,
The ship that has been
Our home on the waves
Comes sailing into the bay.

Jenny Giles

Questions

1. How long can some submarines stay under the water?

2. What do sailors sometimes do to get from one end of an oil tanker to the other?

3. How many planes can some aircraft carriers hold?

Glossary

container	a large tank for storing goods
hold	the place where cargo is put inside a ship
propeller	a set of spinning blades that pushes a boat or plane forward
runway	the place where planes take off and land